Mode

Elegant drape, subtle sheen ... ...me with an ultra soft hand to create an exceptionally versatile yarn. Red Heart® Soft® is ideal for knit and crochet projects for the entire family, from apparel to accents for your home. This book showcasing Red Heart® Soft® presents 12 original motifs by Edie Eckman for you to crochet, plus four fabulous projects to show how they can be used. The pillow, market bag, baby blanket, and throw all can be made in any combination of colors to match your wardrobe or home décor. Let your imagination run free!

LEISURE ARTS, INC.
Maumelle, Arkansas

Flower Hexagon

 **EASY**

Motif measures
8" (20.5 cm) edge-to-edge.

SHOPPING LIST

Yarn (Medium Weight)
RED HEART® Soft®:
- ☐ 2515 Turquoise **A**
- ☐ 9518 Teal **B**
- ☐ 4420 Guacamole **C**

Crochet Hook
- ☐ 6 mm [US J-10]

GAUGE INFORMATION

Rounds 1-6 = 6" (15 cm)
edge-to-edge.
Gauge is not crucial in this pattern.

MOTIF

With **A**, ch 4; join with slip st to form
a ring.

Round 1: Ch 3 (counts as dc), 11 dc
in ring; join with slip st to top of
beginning ch-3 – 12 dc.

Round 2: *Ch 3, (3 tr, ch 3,
slip st) in same st, ch 1, skip
next dc, slip st in next st; repeat
from * around – 6 petals made.
Fasten off **A**.

Round 3: Join **B** with slip st in any
ch-1 space; ch 6 (counts as tr and
ch 2), tr in same space, keeping
Round 2 petals to the front, ch 3,
*(tr, ch 2, tr) in next ch-1 space,
ch 3; repeat from * around; join
with slip st to 4th ch of beginning
ch-6 – 6 ch-3 spaces.

Round 4: Ch 7 (counts as dc and
ch 4), *dc in next tr, ch 1, dc in
next ch-3 space**, ch 1, dc in next
tr, ch 4; repeat from * around,
ending last repeat at **; join with
sc to 3rd ch of beginning ch-7 –
18 dc. Fasten off **B**.

Round 5: Join **C** with sc in same
space *(see Joining With Sc,
page 45)*; *ch 1, working over
Round 4 ch, (2 dc, ch 2, 2 dc) in
Round 3 ch-2 space, [ch 1, sc in
next space] 2 times; repeat from
* around, omitting last sc; join
with slip st to first sc – 24 dc.
Fasten off **C**.

Round 6: Join **B** with dc in previous join *(see Joining With Dc, page 46)*; dc in each st and ch-1 space around, placing (dc, ch 2, dc) in each corner ch-2 space; join with slip st to first dc, slip st in next st – 66 dc. Fasten off **B**.

Round 7: Join **C** with dc in previous join; *ch 1, skip next dc, dc in next dc, ch 1, skip next dc, (dc, ch 2, dc) in corner ch-2 space, [ch 1, skip next dc, dc in next dc] 4 times; repeat from * around, omitting last dc; join with slip st to first dc – 42 dc. Fasten off **C**.

Round 8: Join **B** with sc in previous join; sc in each dc and ch-1 space around, placing (sc, ch 2, sc) in each corner ch-2 space; join with slip st to first sc – 90 sc. Fasten off **B**.

Round 9: Join **C** with sc in any corner ch-2 space; ch 1, sc in same space, *[ch 1, skip next sc, sc in next sc] 7 times, ch 1, skip next sc**, (sc, ch 1, sc) in next ch-2 space; repeat from * around, ending last repeat at **; join with slip st to first sc – 54 sc. Fasten off **C**.

Weave in all ends.

Spoked Wheel

 **EASY**

**Motif measures
8" (20.5 cm) in diameter.**

SHOPPING LIST

Yarn (Medium Weight)
RED HEART® Soft®:

- ☐ 4608 Wine **A**
- ☐ 4604 Navy **B**
- ☐ 4601 Off White **C**

Crochet Hook

- ☐ 6 mm [US J-10]

GAUGE INFORMATION

Rounds 1-7 = 8" (20.5 cm) in diameter.
Gauge is not crucial in this pattern.

——SPECIAL STITCHES——

Spike Double Crochet (spike dc):
Yo, insert hook into st indicated in round below, pull up a loop, [yo and draw through 2 loops] 2 times.

MOTIF

With **A**, ch 4; join with slip st to form a ring.

Round 1: Ch 1, 12 sc in ring; join with slip st to first sc – 12 sc.

Round 2: Ch 3 (counts as dc), 2 dc in same st, ch 1, skip next sc, *3 dc in next sc, ch 1, skip next sc; repeat from * around; join with slip st to top of beginning ch-3 – 18 dc.

Round 3: Ch 3 (counts as dc), dc in next 2 dc, ch 3, *dc in next 3 dc, ch 3; repeat from * around; join with slip st to top of beginning ch-3 – 6 ch-3 spaces. Fasten off **A**.

Round 4: Join **B** with dc in first st *(see Joining With Dc, page 46)*; *2 dc in next dc, dc in next dc, 4 dc in next ch-3 space, dc in next dc; repeat from * around, omitting last dc; join with slip st to first dc – 48 dc. Fasten off **B**.

Round 5: Join **C** with dc in first st; 2 dc in same st, ch 1, skip next 2 dc, 3 dc in next dc, *ch 1, skip next 2 dc**, 3 dc in next dc; repeat from * around, ending last repeat at **; join with slip st to first dc – 16 ch-1 spaces. Fasten off **C**.

Round 6: Join **B** with dc in any ch-1 space; 3 dc in same space, ch 1, *4 dc in next ch-1 space, ch 1; repeat from * around; join with slip st to first dc – 16 4-dc groups. Fasten off **B**.

Round 7: Join **C** with sc in first st *(see Joining With Sc, page 45)*; *sc in next 3 dc, **spike dc** into center dc of 3-dc group in Round 5, sc in next dc; repeat from * around, omitting last sc; join with slip st to first sc. Fasten off **C**.

Weave in all ends.

Bull's Eye Square

 **EASY**

**Motif measures
8½" (21.5 cm) square.**

SHOPPING LIST

Yarn (Medium Weight)
RED HEART® Soft®:
☐ 4422 Tangerine **A**
☐ 4420 Guacamole **B**
Crochet Hook
☐ 6 mm [US J-10]

GAUGE INFORMATION

Rounds 1-4 = 5" (12.5 cm) in diameter. **Gauge is not crucial in this pattern.**

MOTIF

With **A**, ch 4; join with slip st to form a ring.

Round 1: Ch 3 (counts as dc), 11 dc in ring; join with slip st to top of beginning ch-3 – 12 dc. Fasten off **A**.

Round 2: Join **B** with dc in any st *(see Joining With Dc, page 46)*; dc in same st, 2 dc in each dc around; join with slip st to first dc – 24 dc. Fasten off **B**.

Round 3: Join **A** with dc in any st; *2 dc in next dc, dc in next dc; repeat from * around, omitting last dc; join with slip st to first dc – 36 dc. Fasten off **A**.

Round 4: Join **B** with dc in any st; *dc in next dc, 2 dc in next dc, dc in next dc; repeat from * around, omitting last dc; join with slip st to first dc – 48 dc. Fasten off **B**.

Round 5: Join **A** with dc in any st; *dc in next 2 dc, 2 dc in next dc, dc in next dc; repeat from * around, omitting last dc; join with slip st to first dc – 60 dc. Fasten off **A**.

Round 6: Join **B** with dc in any st; *2 dc in next dc, dc in next 4 dc; repeat from * around, omitting last dc; join with slip st to first dc – 72 dc.

Round 7: Ch 2 (counts as hdc), *hdc in next dc, dc in next 5 dc, tr in next 2 dc, 5 tr in next dc, tr in next 2 dc, dc in next 5 dc, hdc in next 2 dc; repeat from * around, omitting last hdc; join with slip st to top of beginning ch-2 – 4 5-tr corners.

Round 8: Ch 1, sc in first 11 sts, 3 sc in corner tr, *sc in next 21 sts, 3 sc in corner tr; repeat from * twice, sc in last 10 sts; join with slip st to first sc – 96 sc. Fasten off **B**.

Weave in all ends.

Lacy Circle

 **EASY**

**Motif measures
8" (20.5 cm) in diameter.**

SHOPPING LIST

Yarn (Medium Weight)
RED HEART® Soft®:
- ☐ 9114 Honey **A**
- ☐ 3720 Lavender **B**

Crochet Hook
- ☐ 6 mm [US J-10]

GAUGE INFORMATION

Rounds 1-7 = 8" (20.5 cm) in diameter. **Gauge is not crucial in this pattern.**

——SPECIAL STITCHES——

**3-Double Crochet Cluster
(3-dc cluster):** Yo, insert hook into next st and pull up a loop, yo, draw through 2 loops, [yo, insert hook into same st and pull up a loop, yo, draw through 2 loops] 2 times, yo, draw through all 4 loops on hook.

**Partial Treble Crochet
(partial tr):** Yo 2 times, insert hook into next st and pull up a loop, [yo and draw through 2 loops] 2 times.

**Partial Double Crochet
(partial dc):** Yo, insert hook into next st and pull up a loop, yo, draw through 2 loops.

MOTIF

With **A**, ch 4; join with slip st to form a ring.

Round 1: Ch 3 (counts as dc), 11 dc in ring; join with slip st to top of beginning ch-3 – 12 dc. Fasten off **A**.

Round 2: Join **B** with slip st in any dc; ch 2, [yo, insert hook into same st and pull up a loop, yo, draw through 2 loops] 2 times, yo and draw through all 3 loops— *beginning 3-dc cluster made*, ch 4, *skip next dc, 3-dc cluster in next dc, ch 4; repeat from * around; join with slip st to top of first cluster – 6 ch-4 spaces. Fasten off **B**.

Round 3: Join **A** with dc in any ch space *(see Joining With Dc, page 46)*; 4 dc in same space, dc in next st, *5 dc in next ch space, dc in next st; repeat from * around; join with slip st to first dc – 36 dc. Fasten off **A**.

Round 4: Join **B** with partial tr in any dc; skip next 2 dc, partial tr in next dc, yo and draw through 3 loops to complete st, ch 3, *partial tr in same dc, skip next 2 dc, partial tr in next dc, yo and draw through 3 loops, ch 3; repeat from * around; join with slip st to first st – 12 ch-3 spaces. Fasten off **B**.

Round 5: Repeat Round 3 – 72 dc.

Round 6: Join **B** with partial dc in any dc; ch 2, skip next 2 dc, dc in next dc, ch 3, *partial dc in same st, skip next 2 dc, partial dc in next dc, yo and draw through 3 loops, ch 3; repeat from * around; join with slip st to first st – 24 ch-3 spaces. Fasten off **B**.

Round 7: Join **A** with sc in any ch-3 space *(see Joining With Sc, page 45)*; 2 sc in same space, ch 1, *3 sc in next ch-3 space, ch 1; repeat from * around; join with slip st to first sc – 72 sc. Fasten off **A**.

Weave in all ends.

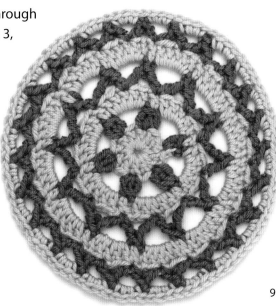

Trinity Shells

**Motif measures
8" (20.5 cm) tip-to-tip.**

SHOPPING LIST

Yarn (Medium Weight)
RED HEART® Soft®:
☐ 9518 Teal **A**
☐ 9520 Seafoam **B**
Crochet Hook
☐ 6 mm [US J-10]

GAUGE INFORMATION

Rounds 1-6 = 8" (20.5 cm) tip-to-tip.
Gauge is not crucial in this pattern.

MOTIF

With **A**, ch 4; join with slip st to form
a ring.

Round 1: Ch 1, [sc in ring, ch 5] 3
times; join with slip st to first sc,
slip st in next space – 3 ch-5 spaces.

Round 2: Ch 2 (counts as hdc),
(9 dc, hdc) in same ch-5 space,
(hdc, 9 dc, hdc) in next
2 ch-5 spaces; join with slip st to
top of beginning ch-2 – 27 dc.
Fasten off **A**.

Round 3: Join **B** with sc *(see
Joining With Sc, page 45)* in
space between any 2 hdc *(Fig. 4,
page 47)*; *ch 3, skip (hdc, 4 dc),
(3 dc, tr, 3 dc) in next dc, ch 3,
sc in space between next 2 hdc;
repeat from * around, omitting
last sc; join with slip st to first sc
– 6 ch-3 spaces.

Round 4: Ch 3 (counts as dc),
4 dc in same sc, *sc in next
ch-3 space, ch 3, skip next 3 dc,
(tr, [ch 1, tr] 4 times) in next tr,
ch 3, sc in next ch-3 space**, 5 dc
in next sc; repeat from * around,
ending last repeat at **; join
with slip st to top of beginning
ch-3, slip st in next 2 dc –
6 ch-3 spaces.

Round 5: Ch 1, sc in same st, *skip next 2 dc, (dc, [ch 1, dc] 2 times) in next sc, sc in next ch-3 space, [ch 1, dc] 2 times in next 4 ch-1 spaces, ch 1, sc in next ch-3 space, (dc, [ch 1, dc] 2 times) in next sc, skip next 2 dc, sc in next dc; repeat from * around, omitting last sc; join with slip st to first sc – 42 dc. Fasten off **B**.

Round 6: Join **A** with *skip next dc, 7 dc in ɪ. next dc, sc in next sc, skip nexɪ ch-1 space, [dc, ch 1] 2 times in next 6 ch-1 spaces, (dc, ch 1, dc) in next ch-1 space, skip next dc, sc in next sc, skip next dc, 5 dc in next dc, skip next dc, sc in next sc; repeat from * around, omitting last sc; join with slip st to first sc – 3 7-dc groups. Fasten off **A**.

Weave in all ends.

11

Openwork Hexagon

Motif measures
8" (20.5 cm) edge-to-edge.

SHOPPING LIST

Yarn (Medium Weight)
RED HEART® Soft®:
- ☐ 9523 Dark Leaf **A**
- ☐ 9518 Teal **B**
- ☐ 3729 Grape **C**

Crochet Hook
- ☐ 6 mm [US J-10]

GAUGE INFORMATION

Rounds 1-7 = 8" (20.5 cm)
edge-to-edge
**Gauge is not crucial in this
pattern.**

MOTIF

With **A**, ch 4; join with slip st to
form a ring.

Round 1: Ch 6 (counts as dc and
ch 3), [dc in ring, ch 3] 5 times; join
with slip st to 3rd ch of beginning
ch-6 – 6 dc. Fasten off **A**.

Round 2: Join **B** with dc in first
ch-3 space *(see Joining With Dc,
page 46)*; 4 dc in same space,
ch 3, *5 dc in next ch-3 space,
ch 3; repeat from * around; join
with slip st to first dc – 30 dc.
Fasten off **B**.

Round 3: Join **C** with dc in any
ch-3 space; 4 dc in same space,
ch 3, *5 dc in next ch-3 space, ch 3;
repeat from * around; join with
slip st to first dc, slip st in next
2 dc – 30 dc.

Round 4: Ch 5 (counts as dc and
ch 2), dc in same st—*beginning
corner space made*, *ch 2, 5 dc
in next ch-3 space, ch 2, skip
next 2 dc**, (dc, ch 2, dc) in next
dc—*corner space made*; repeat
from * around, ending last repeat
at **; join with slip st to 3rd ch
of beginning ch-5 – 6 corners.
Fasten off **C**.

Round 5: Join **A** with dc in any corner ch-2 space; ch 2, dc in same space, *ch 1, dc in next ch-2 space, ch 1, dc in next dc, [ch 1, skip next dc, dc in next dc] 2 times, ch 1, dc in next ch-2 space, ch 1**, (dc, ch 2, dc) in next corner ch-2 space; repeat from * around, ending last repeat at **; join with slip st to first dc – 42 dc. Fasten off **A**.

Round 6: Join **B** with dc in any corner ch-2 space; ch 2, dc in same space, dc in each dc and ch-1 space around, placing (dc, ch 2, dc) in each corner ch-2 space; join with slip st to first dc – 98 dc. Fasten off **B**.

Round 7: Join **C** with sc in any st *(see Joining With Sc, page 45)*; sc in each dc around, placing 2 sc in each corner ch-2 space; join with slip st to first sc – 112 sc. Fasten off **C**.

Weave in all ends.

Elegant Square

 **EASY**

Motif measures
8" (20.5 cm) square.

SHOPPING LIST

Yarn (Medium Weight)
RED HEART® Soft®:
- ☐ 9520 Seafoam **A**
- ☐ 9518 Teal **B**
- ☐ 9523 Dark Leaf **C**

Crochet Hook
- ☐ 6 mm [US J-10]

GAUGE INFORMATION

Rounds 1-6 = 8" (20.5 cm)
edge-to-edge.
**CHECK YOUR GAUGE. Use any
size hook to obtain the gauge.**

——— SPECIAL STITCHES ———

**Double Crochet 2 Together
(dc2tog):** [Yo, insert hook in next
st, yo and pull up loop, yo, draw
through 2 loops] 2 times, yo, draw
through all 3 loops on hook.
**Double Crochet 3 Together
(dc3tog):** [Yo, insert hook in next
st, yo and pull up loop, yo, draw
through 2 loops] 3 times, yo, draw
through all 4 loops on hook.

MOTIF

With **A**, ch 4; join with slip st to
form a ring.

Round 1: Ch 3 (counts as dc), 2 dc
in ring, ch 3, [3 dc in ring, ch 3] 3
times; join with slip st to top of
beginning ch-3 – 12 dc.

Round 2: Ch 2, dc2tog, ch 4, sc
in next ch-3 space, ch 4, *dc3tog,
ch 4, sc in next ch-3 space, ch 4;
repeat from * around; join with
slip st to top of beginning ch-2 –
8 ch-4 spaces. Fasten off **A**.

Round 3: Join **B** with dc in first
ch-4 space *(see Joining With Dc,
page 46)*; 4 dc in same space,

*ch 3, 5 dc in next ch-4 space, ch 1**, 5 dc in next ch-4 space; repeat from * around, ending last repeat at **; join with slip st to first dc – 40 dc. Fasten off **B**.

Round 4: Join **C** with dc in any ch-1 space; 2 dc in same space, *ch 2, skip next 2 dc, sc in next dc, ch 2, skip next 2 dc, (3 dc, ch 3, 3 dc) in next ch-3 space, ch 2, skip next 2 dc, sc in next dc, ch 2, skip next 2 dc**, 3 dc in next ch-1 space; repeat from * around, ending last repeat at **; join with slip st to first dc, slip st in next dc – 36 dc.

Round 5: Ch 4 (counts as dc and ch 1), ([dc, ch 1] 2 times, dc) in same st, *ch 2, sc in next sc, ch 3, (3 dc, ch 3, 3 dc) in next ch-3 space, ch 3, sc in next sc, ch 2, skip next dc**, ([dc, ch 1] 3 times, dc) in next dc; repeat from * around, ending last repeat at **; join with slip st to 3rd ch of beginning ch-4, slip st in next ch-1 space – 40 dc.

Round 6: Ch 4 (coun ch 1), dc in same ch- ch 1, [dc, ch 1] 2 time ch-1 space, *(dc, ch 1, ʋɩ in next ch-1 space, sc in next sc, ch 6, sc in next ch-3 space, ch 3, [3 dc, ch 3] 2 times in next ch-3 space, sc in next ch-3 space, ch 6, sc in next sc, skip next ch-2 space**, [dc, ch 1] 2 times in next 2 ch-1 spaces; repeat from * around, ending last repeat at **; join with slip st to 3rd ch of beginning ch-4 – 8 ch-6 loops. Fasten off **C**.

Weave in all ends.

15

Granny Triangle

 **EASY**

**Motif measures
8" (20.5 cm) corner-to-corner.**

SHOPPING LIST

Yarn (Medium Weight)
RED HEART® Soft®:
- ☐ 2515 Turquoise **A**
- ☐ 9520 Seafoam **B**
- ☐ 4420 Guacamole **C**

Crochet Hook
- ☐ 6 mm [US J-10]

GAUGE INFORMATION
Rounds 1-5 = 8" (20.5 cm)
corner-to-corner.
**CHECK YOUR GAUGE. Use any
size hook to obtain gauge.**

MOTIF
With **A**, ch 4; join with slip st to
form a ring.

Round 1: Ch 3 (counts as dc), 2 dc
in ring, ch 4, *3 dc in ring, ch 4;
repeat from * once more; join with
slip st to top of beginning ch-3 –
9 dc. Fasten off **A**.

Round 2: Join **B** with dc in any
ch-4 space *(see Joining With Dc,
page 46)*; (2 dc, ch 4, 3 dc) in same
space, ch 1, *(3 dc, ch 4, 3 dc) in
next ch-4 space, ch 1; repeat from
* once more; join with slip st to
first dc – 18 dc. Fasten off **B**.

Round 3: Join **C** with dc in any
ch-4 space; (2 dc, ch 4, 3 dc) in
same space, ch 1, 3 dc in next
ch-1 space, ch 1, *(3 dc, ch 4, 3 dc)
in next ch-4 space, ch 1, 3 dc in
next ch-1 space, ch 1; repeat from
* once more; join with slip st to
first dc – 27 dc. Fasten off **C**.

Round 4: Join **B** with dc in any ch-4 space; (2 dc, ch 4, 3 dc) in same space, [ch 1, 3 dc in next ch-1 space] 2 times, ch 1, *(3 dc, ch 4, 3 dc) in next ch-4 space, [ch 1, 3 dc in next ch-1 space] 2 times, ch 1; repeat from * once more; join with slip st to first dc – 36 dc. Fasten off **B**.

Round 5: Join **A** with dc in any ch-4 space; (2 dc, ch 4, 3 dc) in same space, [ch 1, 3 dc in next ch-1 space] 3 times, ch 1, *(3 dc, ch 4, 3 dc) in next ch-4 space, [ch 1, 3 dc in next ch-1 space] 3 times, ch 1; repeat from * once more; join with slip st to first dc – 45 dc. Fasten off **A**.

Round 6: Join **C** with dc in any ch-4 space; (2 dc, ch 4, 3 dc) in same space, [ch 1, 3 dc in next ch-1 space] 4 times, ch 1, *(3 dc, ch 4, 3 dc) in next ch-4 space, [ch 1, 3 dc in next ch-1 space] 4 times, ch 1; repeat from * once more; join with slip st to first dc – 54 dc. Fasten off **C**.

Weave in all ends.

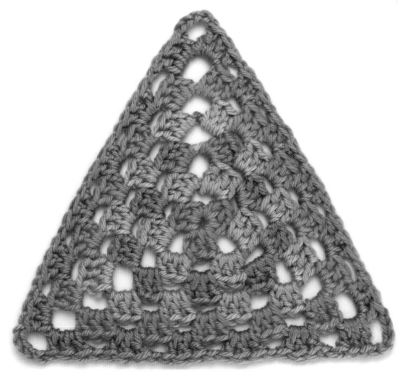

Chain-Flower Granny

 **EASY**

**Motif measures
7½" (19 cm) square.**

SHOPPING LIST

Yarn (Medium Weight)
RED HEART® Soft®:
- ☐ 4600 White **A**
- ☐ 2515 Turquoise **B**
- ☐ 4420 Guacamole **C**

Crochet Hook
- ☐ 6 mm [US J-10]

GAUGE INFORMATION
Rounds 1-9 = 7½" (19 cm) square.
**CHECK YOUR GAUGE. Use any
size hook to obtain gauge.**

MOTIF
With **A**, ch 5; join with slip st to
form a ring.

Round 1: Ch 1, [sc in ring, ch 5] 8
times; join with slip st to first sc –
8 sc. Fasten off **A**.

Round 2: Join **B** with sc *(see Joining
With Sc, page 45)* in front loop only
of any sc *(Fig. 2, page 46)*; ch 5,
*sc in front loop only of next sc,
ch 5; repeat from * around; join
with slip st to first sc – 8 sc and
8 ch-5 loops. Fasten off **B**.

Round 3: Join **C** with sc in the back
loop of any Round 1 sc; *ch 1, sc in
back loop of next Round 1 sc**, ch 3,
sc in back loop of next Round 1 sc;
repeat from * around, ending last
repeat at **; join with dc in first sc –
4 ch-3 corners.

Round 4: Ch 3 (counts as dc), (2 dc,
ch 2, 3 dc) in same space, ch 1, 3 dc
in next ch-1 space, *ch 1, (3 dc,
ch 2, 3 dc) in next ch-3 space, ch 1,
3 dc in next ch-1 space; repeat
from * around; join with sc in top of
beginning ch-3 – 36 dc.

Round 5: Ch 3 (counts as dc), 2 dc in
same space, *ch 1, (3 dc, ch 2, 3 dc)
in next ch-2 space**, [ch 1, 3 dc in
next ch-1 space] 2 times; repeat
from * around, ending last repeat
at **, ch 1, 3 dc in next ch-1 space,
ch 1; join with slip st to top of
beginning ch-3 – 48 dc. Fasten off **C**.

Round 6: Join **B** with sc in any Round 3 sc; ch 7, [sc in next Round 3 sc, ch 7] 7 times; join with slip st to first sc – 8 ch-7 loops. Fasten off **B**.

Round 7: Join **A** with dc in any ch-2 space of Round 5 *(see Joining With Dc, page 46)*; (2 dc, ch 2, 3 dc) in same space, *[ch 1, 3 dc in next ch-1 space] 3 times, ch 1**, (3 dc, ch 2, 3 dc) in next ch-2 space; repeat from * around, ending last repeat at **; join with slip st to first dc – 60 dc. Fasten off **A**.

Round 8: Join **C** with dc in any ch-2 space; (2 dc, ch 2, 3 dc) in same space, *[ch 1, 3 dc in next ch-1 space] 4 times**, ch 1, (3 dc, ch 2, 3 dc) in next ch-2 space, repeat from * around, ending last repeat at **; join with sc to first dc – 72 dc.

Round 9: Ch 3 (counts as dc), 2 dc in same st, ch 1, *(3 dc, ch 2, 3 dc) in next ch-2 space, ch 1**, [3 dc in next ch-1 space, ch 1] 5 times; repeat from * around, ending last repeat at **, [3 dc in next ch-1 space, ch 1] 4 times; join with slip st to top of beginning ch-3 – 84 dc. Fasten off **C**.

Weave in all ends.

Square Medallion

 **EASY**

Motif measures
8" (20.5 cm) square.

SHOPPING LIST

Yarn (Medium Weight)
RED HEART® Soft®:
- ☐ 4601 Off White **A**
- ☐ 9518 Teal **B**
- ☐ 9440 Light Grey Heather **C**

Crochet Hook
- ☐ 6 mm [US J-10]

GAUGE INFORMATION

Rounds 1-10 = 8" (20.5 cm) square, blocked.
Gauge is not crucial in this pattern.

——— SPECIAL STITCHES ———

Double Crochet 2 Together (dc2tog): [Yo, insert hook in next st, yo and pull up loop, yo, draw through 2 loops] 2 times, yo, draw through all 3 loops on hook.
Double Crochet 3 Together (dc3tog): [Yo, insert hook in next st, yo and pull up loop, yo, draw through 2 loops] 3 times, yo, draw through all 4 loops on hook.

MOTIF

With **A**, ch 4; join with slip st to form a ring.

Round 1: Ch 1, 8 sc in ring; join with slip st to first sc – 8 sc.

Round 2: Ch 3 (counts as dc), 2 dc in same st, [ch 3, skip next sc, 3 dc in next sc] 3 times, ch 3, skip next sc; join with slip st to top of beginning ch-3 – 12 dc.

Round 3: Ch 2, dc2tog over next 2 dc, *ch 3, (sc, ch 3, sc) in next ch-3 space, ch 3**, dc3tog over next 3 dc; repeat from * around, ending last repeat at **; join with slip st to top of beginning ch-2 – 4 clusters. Fasten off **A**.

Round 4: Join **B** with sc in first st *(see Joining With Sc, page 45)*; *ch 5, skip next ch-3 space, (sc, ch 5, sc) in corner ch-3 space**, ch 5, sc in next cluster; repeat from * around, ending last repeat at **, ch 5; join with slip st to first sc – 12 ch-5 spaces. Fasten off **B**.

Round 5: Join **C** with sc in previous ch-5 space; *ch 5, sc in next ch-5 space, ch 5, (sc, ch 5, sc) in corner ch-5 space**, ch 5, sc in next ch-5 space; repeat from * around, ending last repeat at **, ch 2; join with dc in first sc – 16 ch-5 spaces.

Round 6: Ch 1, sc in same ch-5 space, *ch 5, sc in next ch-5 space; repeat from * around, ending with ch 2; join with dc in first sc – 16 ch-5 spaces.

Round 7: Ch 1, sc in same ch-5 space, *ch 6, sc in next ch-5 space; repeat from * around, ending with ch 2; join with tr in first sc – 16 ch-6 spaces.

(Instructions continue on page 44)

Navy Octagon

 **EASY**

Motif measures
8" (20.5 cm) in diameter.

SHOPPING LIST

Yarn (Medium Weight)
RED HEART® Soft®:
- ☐ 9344 Chocolate **A**
- ☐ 4608 Wine **B**
- ☐ 4604 Navy **C**

Crochet Hook
- ☐ 6 mm [US J-10]

GAUGE INFORMATION
Rounds 1-7 = 8" (20.5 cm)
diameter. **Gauge is not crucial in
this pattern.**

—SPECIAL STITCHES—
**2 Double Crochet Cluster
(2-dc cluster):** [Yo, insert hook
into st or space indicated and
pull up a loop, yo, draw through
2 loops] 2 times, yo and draw
through all 3 loops on hook.
Spike Single Crochet (spike sc):
Sc in space in round below next st.

MOTIF
With **A**, ch 6; join with slip st to
form a ring.

Round 1: Ch 2, dc in ring, ch 2,
[2-dc cluster in ring, ch 2] 7
times; join with slip st to first dc –
8 clusters. Fasten off **A**.

Round 2: With **B**, beginning with
slip knot on hook, (2-dc cluster,
ch 2, 2-dc cluster, ch 1) in each
ch-2 space around; join with slip st
to top of first cluster – 16 clusters.
Fasten off **B**.

Round 3: Join **C** with sc in any ch-1 space *(see Joining With Sc, page 45)*; *sc in next cluster, (spike sc, ch 2, spike sc) in next Round 1 ch-2 space, sc in next cluster, sc in next ch-1 space; repeat from * around, omitting last sc; join with slip st to first sc – 16 spike sc. Fasten off **C**.

Round 4: Join **A** with dc in first sc *(see Joining With Dc, page 46)*; dc in next 2 sc, ch 2, *dc in next 5 sc, ch 2; repeat from * around, ending with dc in last 2 sc; join with slip st to first dc – 40 dc. Fasten off **A**.

Round 5: Join **C** with dc ch 1, skip next 2 dc, *(2-dc ch 3, 2-dc cluster) in next ch-2 space, ch 1**, skip next 2 dc, dc in next dc, ch 1, skip next 2 dc; repeat from * around, ending last repeat at **; join with slip st to first dc – 16 clusters.

Round 6: Ch 4 (counts as dc and ch 1), dc in same dc, *ch 2, skip next (ch 1, cluster), (2-dc cluster, ch 3, 2-dc cluster) in next ch-3 space, ch 2, skip next (cluster, ch 1)**, (dc, ch 1, dc) in next dc; repeat from * around, ending last repeat at **; join with slip st to 3rd ch of beginning ch-4 – 16 clusters.

(Instructions continue on page 44)

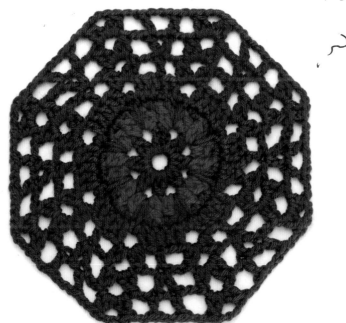

Rounded Square

 **EASY**

**Motif measures
8" (20.5 cm) in diameter.**

SHOPPING LIST

Yarn (Medium Weight)
RED HEART® Soft®:
- ☐ 9523 Dark Leaf **A**
- ☐ 4601 Off White **B**

Crochet Hook
- ☐ 6 mm [US J-10]

GAUGE INFORMATION

Rounds 1-8 = 8" (20.5 cm) diameter.
Gauge is not crucial in this pattern.

———— SPECIAL STITCHES ————

**2 Double Crochet Cluster
(2-dc cluster):** [Yo, insert hook into
st or space indicated and pull up a
loop, yo, draw through 2 loops] 2
times, yo and draw through all
3 loops on hook.
Spike Single Crochet (spike sc): Sc
in space in round below next st.

MOTIF

With **A**, ch 4; join with slip st to
form a ring.

Round 1: Ch 2, dc in ring, ch 4, tr
in 4th ch from hook, *2-dc cluster
in ring, ch 4, tr in 4th ch from
hook; repeat from * 2 times
more; join with slip st to first dc –
4 clusters. Fasten off **A**.

Round 2: Join **B** with sc in any
cluster *(see Joining With Sc,
page 45)*; *[ch 1, dc] 5 times in
next ch-4 space, ch 1, sc in next
cluster; repeat from * around,
omitting last sc; join with slip st
to first sc – 20 dc. Fasten off **B**.

Round 3: Join **A** with sc in any
sc; *ch 3, skip next ch-1 space,
[2-dc cluster in next ch-1 space,
ch 3] 4 times, skip next ch-1 space,
sc in next sc; repeat from * around,
omitting last sc; join with slip st to
first sc – 16 clusters. Fasten off **A**.

Round 4: Join **B** with sc in any sc;
*[ch 3, sc in next cluster] 4 times,
ch 3, sc in next sc; repeat from *
around, omitting last sc; join with
slip st to first sc – 20 sc.

Round 5: Ch 5 (counts as dc and ch 2), *sc in next sc, ch 3, hdc in next sc, ch 5, hdc in next sc, ch 3, sc in next sc, ch 2**, dc in next sc, ch 2; repeat from * around, ending last repeat at **; join with slip st to 3rd ch of beginning ch-5 – 8 hdc.

Round 6: Ch 1, sc in same st, *ch 2, sc in next sc, ch 3, sc in next hdc, ch 3, [sc, ch 3] 2 times in next ch-5 space, sc in next hdc, ch 3, sc in next sc, ch 2, sc in next dc; repeat from * around, omitting last sc; join with slip st to first sc – 28 sc.

Round 7: Ch 3 (counts as *2 dc in next ch-2 space, d next sc, [3 dc in next ch-3 space, dc in next sc] 2 times, (dc, ch 1, dc) in next ch-3 space, dc in next sc, [3 dc in next ch-3 space, dc in next sc] 2 times, 2 dc in next ch-2 space, dc in next sc; repeat from * around, omitting last dc; join with slip st to top of beginning ch-3 – 100 dc. Fasten off **B**.

(Instructions continue on page 44)

BULL'S EYE SQUARE PILLOW

Put 8 squares together to make a pillow! It's a simple idea for adding a graphic accent to a modern bedroom or living area.

 **EASY**

Pillow measures 20" (51 cm) square.

SHOPPING LIST

Yarn (Medium Weight) 🧶 **4**
RED HEART® Soft®:
- ☐ 4422 Tangerine **A** - 1 ball
- ☐ 4420 Guacamole **B** - 1 ball

Crochet Hook
- ☐ 6 mm [US J-10]

Additional Supplies
- ☐ 20" (51 cm) square pillow form

GAUGE INFORMATION
Rounds 1-4 = 5" (12.5 cm) diameter.
CHECK YOUR GAUGE. Use any size hook to obtain gauge.

MOTIF (Make 8)
With **A**, ch 4; join with slip st to form a ring.

Round 1 (Right side): Ch 3 (counts as dc), 11 dc in ring; join with slip st to top of beginning ch-3 – 12 dc. Fasten off **A**.

Round 2: Join **B** with dc in any st *(see Joining With Dc, page 46)*; dc in same st, 2 dc in each dc around; join with slip st to first dc – 24 dc. Fasten off **B**.

Round 3: Join **A** with dc in any st; *2 dc in next dc, dc in next dc; repeat from * around, omitting last dc; join with slip st to first dc – 36 dc. Fasten off **A**.

Round 4: Join **B** with dc in any st; *dc in next dc, 2 dc in next dc, dc in next dc; repeat from * around, omitting last dc; join with slip st to first dc – 48 dc. Fasten off **B**.

Round 5: Join **A** with dc in any st; *dc in next 2 dc, 2 dc in next dc, dc in next dc; repeat from * around, omitting last dc; join with slip st to first dc – 60 dc. Fasten off **A**.

Round 6: Join **B** with dc in any st; *2 dc in next dc, dc in next 4 dc; repeat from * around, omitting last dc; join with slip st to first dc – 72 dc.

Round 7: Ch 2 (counts as hdc), *hdc in next dc, dc in next 5 dc, tr in next 2 dc, 5 tr in next dc, tr in next 2 dc, dc in next 5 dc, hdc in next 2 dc; repeat from * around, omitting last hdc; join with slip st to top of beginning ch-2 – 4 5-tr corners.

Round 8: Ch 1, sc in next 11 sts, 3 sc in corner tr, *sc in next 21 sts, 3 sc in corner tr; repeat from * twice, sc in last 10 sts; join with slip st to first sc – 96 sc. Fasten off **B**.

PILLOW

Side 1 – Pillow Back
Place 4 motifs in a 2 x 2 arrangement. Holding squares with right sides together, with **B**, sc through each pair of adjacent sts to join all four squares. Fasten off. Repeat for other (perpendicular) seam, but do not fasten off.

Border
Round 1: Ch 3 (counts as dc), *dc in each st to corner, (2 dc, tr, 2 dc) in corner st; repeat from * 3 times, dc in each st to beginning, changing to **A** in last st *(Fig. 3, page 47)*; join with slip st to top of beginning ch-3.

Round 2: Ch 3 (counts as dc), *dc in each st to corner, 3 dc in corner tr; repeat from * 3 times, dc in each st to beginning, changing to **B** in last st; join with slip st to top of beginning ch-3.

Round 3: Ch 3 (counts as dc), *dc in each st to corner, (2 dc, tr, 2 dc) in corner st; repeat from * 3 times, dc in each st to beginning; join with slip st to top of beginning ch-3. Fasten off **B**.

Side 2 – Pillow Front
Make as for Side 1; do not fasten off at the end of Border Round 3.

FINISHING

Holding front and back with wrong sides together, ch 1, sc through each pair of adjacent sts around 3 sides, placing 3 sc in each corner st; insert pillow form, then continue working through both layers to beginning; join with slip st to first sc. Fasten off **B**.

Weave in all ends.

SQUARE MEDALLION MARKET BAG

Shown on page 30.

Would you rather not have to sew motifs together? These squares are joined together during the last round of the square. Just follow the pattern for all 10 rounds of the first square and then join each new square to previous squares as you do Round 10.

 **EASY**

Bag measures
16" wide x 16½" high (40.5 cm x 42 cm), excluding handles.

SHOPPING LIST

Yarn (Medium Weight) 4
RED HEART® Soft®:
- [ ] 4601 Off White **A** - 1 ball
- [ ] 9518 Teal **B** - 1 ball
- [ ] 9440 Light Grey Heather **B** - 1 ball
   Note: Use Teal for B in 4 motifs & Light Grey Heather for B in 4 motifs

Crochet Hook
- [ ] 6 mm [US J-10]

GAUGE INFORMATION
Rounds 1-10 = 8" (20.5 cm) diameter, blocked.
Gauge is not crucial in this pattern.

── SPECIAL STITCHES ──

**Double Crochet 2 Together
(dc2tog):** [Yo, insert hook in next st, yo and pull up loop, yo, draw through 2 loops] 2 times, yo, draw through all 3 loops on hook.

**Double Crochet 3 Together
(dc3tog):** [Yo, insert hook in next st, yo and pull up loop, yo, draw through 2 loops] 3 times, yo, draw through all 4 loops on hook.

MOTIF (Make 4 with Teal for B & 4 with Light Grey Heather for B)

With **A**, ch 4; join with slip st to form a ring.

Round 1 (Right side): Ch 1, 8 sc in ring; join with slip st to first sc – 8 sc.

Round 2: Ch 3 (counts as dc), 2 dc in same st, [ch 3, skip next sc, 3 dc in next sc] 3 times, ch 3, skip next sc; join with slip st to top of beginning ch-3 – 12 dc.

Round 3: Ch 2, dc2tog over next 2 dc, *ch 3, [sc, ch 3, sc] in next ch-3 space, ch 3**, dc3tog over next 3 dc; repeat from * around, ending last repeat at **; join with slip st to top of beginning ch-2 – 4 clusters. Fasten off **A**.

Round 4: Join **B** with sc in first st *(see Joining With Sc, page 45)*; *ch 5, skip next ch-3 space, (sc, ch 5, sc) in corner ch-3 space**, ch 5, sc in next cluster; repeat from * around, ending last repeat at **, ch 2; join with dc to first sc – 12 ch-5 spaces.

Round 5: Ch 1, sc in same ch-5 space, *ch 5, sc in next ch-5 space, ch 5, (sc, ch 5, sc) in corner ch-5 space**, ch 5, sc in next ch-5 space; repeat from * around, ending last repeat at **, ch 2; join with dc in first sc – 16 ch-5 spaces.

Round 6: Ch 1, sc in same ch-5 space, *ch 5, sc in next ch-5 space; repeat from * around, ending with ch 2; join with dc in first sc – 16 ch-5 spaces.

Round 7: Ch 1, sc in same ch-5 space, *ch 6, sc in next ch-5 space; repeat from * around, ending with ch 2; join with tr in first sc – 16 ch-6 spaces.

Round 8: Ch 1, (sc, ch 5, sc) in same ch-6 space, *[ch 5, sc in next ch-6 space] 3 times, [ch 5, sc] 2 times in next ch-6 space; repeat from * around, ending with [ch 5, sc in next ch-6 space] 3 times, ch 2; join with dc to first sc – 20 ch-5 spaces.

Round 9: Ch 1, sc in same ch-5 space, ch 5, *[sc, ch 5] 2 times in corner ch-5 space**, [sc in next ch-5 space, ch 5] 4 times; repeat from * around, ending last repeat at **, [sc in next ch-5 space, ch 5] 2 times, sc in next ch-5 space, ch 2; join with dc to first sc – 24 ch-5 spaces.

Round 10: Ch 1, sc in same ch-5 space, ch 3, sc in next ch-5 space, ch 3, *[sc, ch 3] 2 times in corner ch-5 space**, [sc in next ch-5 space, ch 3] 5 times; repeat from * around, ending last repeat with [sc in next ch-5 space, ch 3] 3 times; join with slip st to first sc – 28 ch-3 spaces. Fasten off **B**.

BAG

Make first Motif through Round 10.

Referring to Assembly Diagram for yarn colors and motif placement, make Motif 2 through Round 9; join Motif 2 to Motif 1 as follows:

Round 10 (Joining round): Ch 1, sc in same ch-5 space, ch 3, sc in next ch-5 space, *[ch 3, sc] 2 times in corner ch-5 space, [ch 3, sc in next ch-5 space] 5 times; repeat from * once, ch 3, sc in corner ch-5 space, ch 1, sc in corner ch-5 space of previous motif, ch 1, sc in same corner ch-5 space of current motif, [ch 1, sc in adjacent ch-5 space of previous motif, ch 1, sc in next ch-5 space of current motif] 5 times, ch 1, sc in adjacent ch-5 space of previous motif, ch 1, sc in corner ch-5 space of current motif, ch 1, sc in corner ch-5 space of previous motif, ch 1, sc in same ch-5 corner space of current motif, [ch 3, sc in next ch-5 space] 3 times, ch 3; join with slip st to first sc. Fasten off **B**.

Referring to Assembly Diagram for placement of colors and squares, make and join Motifs 3, 4, 5, and 6.

For the last 2 motifs (7 and 8), join them to the previous motifs and also to the first two motifs to form a tube.

Assembly Diagram

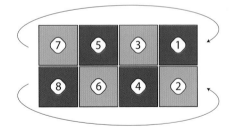

Finishing

Bottom Seam: Turn bag inside out and flatten into a double-layered 2 x 2 square. With right sides together and wrong side facing, join **B** with sc through both corner spaces of one edge. Working through both layers, [ch 1, 3 sc in next ch-3 space] 6 times, ch 1, sc in next ch-3 space, [ch 1, 3 sc in next ch-3 space] 6 times, ch 1, sc in last ch-3 space. Fasten off **B**.

Edging and handles: Turn bag right side out.

Round 1: Working around top of bag and with right side facing, join **B** with sc in first corner space at upper right corner; *[ch 1, sc] 2 times in next 6 ch-3 spaces**, [ch 1, sc in next ch-3 space] 2 times; repeat from * around, ending last repeat at **, ch 1, sc in next ch-3 space; join with sc to first sc – 112 sts.

Round 2: Ch 1, sc in same space, *ch 1, sc in next ch-1 space; repeat from * around, ending join with sc to first sc – 112 sts.

Round 3: Ch 1, sc in same ch-1 space, [ch 1, sc in next ch-1 space] 8 times, *sc in next sc, ch 49 for handle, skip next 23 sts, sc in next sc**, sc in next ch-1 space, [ch 1, sc in next ch-1 space] 15 times; repeat from * to ** once, [sc in next ch-1 space, ch 1] 6 times, sc in next ch-1 space; join with sc to first sc – 163 sts.

Round 4: Ch 1, sc in same ch-1 space, *[ch 1, sc in next ch-1 space] 8 times, ch 1, skip next sc, sc in next sc, [ch 1, skip next ch, sc in back bar of next ch *(Fig. 1, page 46)*] 24 times, ch 1, skip next ch, sc in next sc**, [ch 1, sc in next ch-1 space] 7 times; repeat from * to ** once, [ch 1, sc in next ch-1 space] 6 times; join with sc to first sc – 163 sts.

Round 5: Ch 1, sc in same ch-1 space, *ch 1, sc in next ch-1 space; repeat from * around; join with slip st to first sc – 163 sts. Fasten off **B**.

Weave in all ends.

CHAIN-FLOWER GRANNY BABY BLANKET

Whether you make this blanket in bright colors or pastels, it is a wonderful comfort to a baby or toddler. There are just 16 motifs joined together while crocheting the last round.

 **EASY**

Blanket measures 35" (89 cm) square.

SHOPPING LIST

Yarn (Medium Weight) **4**
RED HEART® Soft®:
- ☐ 4600 White **A** - 1 ball
- ☐ 2515 Turquoise **B** - 1 ball
- ☐ 4420 Guacamole **C** - 1 ball

Crochet Hook
- ☐ 6 mm [US J-10]

GAUGE INFORMATION

Rounds 1-9 = 7½" (19 cm) square.
CHECK YOUR GAUGE. Use any size hook to obtain the gauge.

MOTIF

With **A**, ch 5; join with slip st to form a ring.

Round 1: Ch 1, [sc in ring, ch 5] 8 times; join with slip st to first sc – 8 sc. Fasten off **A**.

Round 2: Join **B** with sc *(see Joining With Sc, page 45)* in front loop only of any sc *(Fig. 2, page 46)*; ch 5, *sc in front loop only of next sc, ch 5; repeat from * around; join with slip st to first sc – 8 sc and 8 ch-5 loops. Fasten off **B**.

Round 3: Join **C** with sc in the back loop of any Round 1 sc; *ch 1, sc in back loop of next Round 1 sc**, ch 3, sc in back loop of next Round 1 sc; repeat from * around, ending last repeat at **; join with dc in first sc – 4 ch-3 corners.

Round 4: Ch 3 (counts as dc), (2 dc, ch 2, 3 dc) in same space, ch 1, 3 dc in next ch-1 space, *ch 1, (3 dc, ch 2, 3 dc) in next ch-3 space, ch 1, 3 dc in next ch-1 space; repeat from * around; join with sc in top of beginning ch-3 – 36 dc.

Round 5: Ch 3 (counts as dc), 2 dc in same space, *ch 1, (3 dc, ch 2, 3 dc) in next ch-2 space**, [ch 1, 3 dc in next ch-1 space] 2 times; repeat from * around, ending last repeat at **, ch 1, 3 dc in next ch-1 space, ch 1; join with slip st to top of beginning ch-3 – 48 dc. Fasten off **C**.

Round 6: Join **B** with sc in any Round 3 sc; ch 7, [sc in next Round 3 sc, ch 7] 7 times; join with slip st to first sc – 8 ch-7 loops. Fasten off **B**.

Round 7: Join **A** with dc in any ch-2 space of Round 5 *(see Joining With Dc, page 46)*; (2 dc, ch 2, 3 dc) in same space, *[ch 1, 3 dc in next ch-1 space] 3 times, ch 1**, (3 dc, ch 2, 3 dc) in next ch-2 space; repeat from * around, ending last repeat at **; join with slip st to first dc – 60 dc. Fasten off **A**.

Round 8: Join **C** with dc in any ch-2 space; (2 dc, ch 2, 3 dc) in same space, *[ch 1, 3 dc in next ch-1 space] 4 times**, ch 1, (3 dc, ch 2, 3 dc) in next ch-2 space; repeat from * around, ending last repeat at **; join with sc to first dc – 72 dc.

Round 9: Ch 3 (counts as dc), 2 dc in same st, ch 1, *(3 dc, ch 2, 3 dc) in next ch-2 space, ch 1**, [3 dc in next ch-1 space, ch 1] 5 times; repeat from * around, ending last repeat at **, [3 dc in next ch-1 space, ch 1] 4 times; join with slip st to top of beginning ch-3 – 84 dc. Fasten off **C**.

Round 9 (Joining round): Ch 3 (counts as dc), 2 dc in same space, ch 1, *(3 dc, ch 2, 3 dc) in next ch-2 space, ch 1**, [3 dc in next ch-1 space, ch 1] 5 times; repeat from * once, (3 dc, ch 1, slip st in adjacent corner ch-2 space of previous motif, 3 dc) in next ch-2 space, ch 1, [3 dc in next ch-1 space, slip st in adjacent ch-1 space of previous motif] 5 times, (3 dc, ch 1, slip st in adjacent corner ch-2 space of previous motif, 3 dc) in next ch-2 space, ch 1, [3 dc in next ch-1 space, ch 1] 4 times; join with slip st to top of beginning ch-3 – 84 dc. Fasten off **C**.

BLANKET

Make one Chain-Flower Granny Motif. Make 15 additional Motifs through Round 8; referring to Assembly Diagram, join Motifs in a 4 x 4 arrangement as follows:

Assembly Diagram

Border

Round 1: Join **C** with sc in any corner ch-2 space; *[ch 1, skip next dc, sc in next dc, ch 1, skip next dc, sc in next ch-1 space] 7 times**, ch 1, sc in same ch-1 space; repeat from * 2 times, repeat from * to ** once, [sc, ch 1, sc] in corner ch-1 space; repeat from * 3 times, omitting last [sc, ch 1, sc]; join with slip st to first sc – 240 sc. Fasten off **C**.

Round 2: Join **A** with sc in any corner ch-1 space; *ch 1, 3 dc in next ch-1 space, [sc in next ch-1 space, 3 dc in next ch-1 space] to corner, ch 1, sc in corner ch-1 space; repeat from * around, omitting last sc; join with slip st to first sc – 120 3-dc groups. Fasten off **A**.

Round 3: Join **C** with dc in any corner sc; 6 dc in same st, *skip next dc, sc in next dc, [skip next dc, 3 dc in next sc, skip next dc, sc in next dc] 29 times**, 7 dc in corner sc; repeat from * around, ending last repeat at **; join with slip st to first dc – 116 3-dc groups. Fasten off **C**.

Round 4: Join **B** with sc in any sc; ch 3, skip next st, *sc in next st, ch 3, skip next st; repeat from * around; join with slip st to first sc. Fasten off **B**.

Weave in all ends.

ELEGANT SQUARES THROW

Shown on page 41.

The granny is all grown up and elegant in these stylish home décor colors. You'll love joining the motifs to each other during the last round, so that you don't have to sew them all together.

 **EASY**

Throw measures 40" x 48" (101.5 cm x 122 cm).

SHOPPING LIST

Yarn (Medium Weight)

RED HEART® Soft®:

- ☐ 2515 Turquoise **A** - 1 ball
- ☐ 9518 Teal **B** - 1 ball
- ☐ 4420 Guacamole **C** - 1 ball
- ☐ 4614 Black **D** - 1 ball
- ☐ 9520 Seafoam **E** - 1 ball
- ☐ 9440 Light Grey Heather **F** - 1 ball
- ☐ 9523 Dark Leaf **G** - 1 ball

Crochet Hook

- ☐ 5.5 mm [US I-9]

GAUGE INFORMATION

Motif Rounds 1-6 = 8" (20.5 cm) edge-to-edge.

CHECK YOUR GAUGE. Use any size hook to obtain gauge.

─── SPECIAL STITCHES ───

Double Crochet 2 Together (dc2tog): [Yo, insert hook in next st, yo and pull up loop, yo, draw through 2 loops] 2 times, yo, draw through all 3 loops on hook.

Double Crochet 3 Together (dc3tog): [Yo, insert hook in next st, yo and pull up loop, yo, draw through 2 loops] 3 times, yo, draw through all 4 loops on hook.

NOTES: Squares are joined using a join-as-you-go method to minimize finishing tasks. If you prefer, make 30 individual square motifs and crochet or sew them together later.

MOTIF

With **first color**, ch 4; join with slip st to form a ring.

Round 1: Ch 3 (counts as dc), 2 dc in ring, ch 3, [3 dc in ring, ch 3] 3 times; join with slip st to top of beginning ch-3 – 12 dc.

Round 2: Ch 2, dc2tog, ch 4, sc in next ch-3 space, ch 4, *dc3tog, ch 4, sc in next ch-3 space, ch 4; repeat from * around; join with slip st to top of beginning ch-2 – 8 ch-4 spaces. Fasten off **first color**.

Round 3: Join **second color** with dc in first ch-4 space *(see Joining With Dc, page 46)*; 4 dc in same space, *ch 3, 5 dc in next ch-4 space, ch 1**, 5 dc in next ch-4 space; repeat from * around, ending last repeat at **; join with slip st to first dc – 40 dc. Fasten off **second color**.

Round 4: Join **third color** with dc in any ch-1 space; 2 dc in same space, *ch 2, skip next 2 dc, sc in next dc, ch 2, skip next 2 dc, (3 dc, ch 3, 3 dc) in next ch-3 space, ch 2, skip next 2 dc, sc in next dc, ch 2, skip next 2 dc**, 3 dc in next ch-1 space; repeat from * around, ending last repeat at **; join with slip st to first dc, slip st in next dc – 36 dc.

Round 5: Ch 4 (counts as dc and ch 1), ([dc, ch 1] 2 times, dc) in same st, *ch 2, sc in next sc, ch 3, (3 dc, ch 3, 3 dc) in next ch-3 space, ch 3, sc in next sc, ch 2, skip next dc**, ([dc, ch 1] 3 times, dc) in next dc; repeat from * around, ending last repeat at **; join with slip st to 3rd ch of beginning ch-4, slip st in next space – 40 dc.

Round 6: Ch 4 (counts as dc and ch 1), dc in same ch-1 space, ch 1, [dc, ch 1] 2 times in next ch-1 space, *(dc, ch 1, dc) in next ch-1 space, sc in next sc, ch 6, sc in next ch-3 space, ch 3, [3 dc, ch 3] 2 times in next ch-3 space, sc in next ch-3 space, ch 6, sc in next sc, skip next ch-2 space**, [dc, ch 1] 2 times in next 2 ch-1 spaces; repeat from * around, ending last repeat at **; join with slip st to 3rd ch of beginning ch-4 – 8 ch-6 loops. Fasten off **third color**.

THROW

Referring to Assembly Diagram for colors and placement of motifs, make one Elegant Square Motif through Round 6. Make subsequent Motifs through Round 5; join to previous square as follows:

Round 6 (Joining round): Ch 4 (counts as dc and ch 1), dc in same ch-1 space, ch 1, [dc, ch 1] 2 times in next ch-1 space, *(dc, ch 1, dc) in next ch-1 space, sc in next sc, ch 6, sc in next ch-3 space, ch 3, [3 dc, ch 3] 2 times in next ch-3 space, sc in next ch-3 space, ch 6, sc in next sc, skip next ch-2 space, [dc, ch 1] 2 times in next 2 ch-1 spaces; repeat from * once, (dc, ch 1, dc) in next ch-1 space, sc in next sc, ch 6, sc in next ch-3 space, ch 3, 3 dc in next ch-3 space, ch 1, sc in corner ch-3 space of adjacent motif, ch 1, 3 dc in same ch-3 space, ch 3, sc in next ch-3 space, ch 3, sc in ch-6 loop of adjacent motif, ch 3, sc in next sc, [dc, ch 1] 2 times in next ch-1 space, dc in next ch-1 space, sc in center ch-1 space of adjacent motif, dc in same ch-1 space, ch 1, (dc, ch 1, dc) in next ch-1 space, sc in next sc, ch 3, sc in ch-6 loop of adjacent motif, ch 3, sc in next ch-3 space, ch 3, 3 dc in next ch-3 space, ch 1, sc in corner ch-3 space of adjacent motif, ch 1, 3 dc in same ch-3 space, ch 3, sc in next ch-3 space, ch 6, sc in next sc; join with slip st to 3rd ch of beginning ch-4 – 8 ch-6 loops. Fasten off.

Continue making and joining motifs in a 5 x 6 layout as indicated on Assembly Diagram.

Weave in all ends.

Assembly Diagram

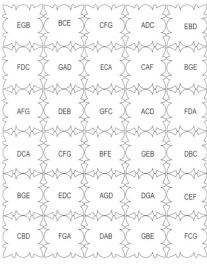

EGB	BCE	CFG	ADC	EBD
FDC	GAD	ECA	CAF	BGE
AFG	DEB	GFC	ACD	FDA
DCA	CFG	BFE	GEB	DBC
BGE	EDC	AGD	DGA	CEF
CBD	FGA	DAB	GBE	FCG

Letters indicate yarn colors in the order they are used in each square

SQUARE MEDALLION
(continued from page 21)

Round 8: Ch 1, (sc, ch 5, sc) in same ch-6 space, *[ch 5, sc in next ch-6 space] 3 times, [ch 5, sc] 2 times in next ch-6 space; repeat from * around, ending with [ch 5, sc in next ch-6 space] 3 times, ch 2; join with dc to first sc – 20 ch-5 spaces.

Round 9: Ch 1, sc in same ch-5 space, ch 5, *[sc, ch 5] 2 times in corner ch-5 space**, [sc in next ch-5 space, ch 5] 4 times; repeat from * around, ending last repeat at **, [sc in next ch-5 space, ch 5] 2 times, sc in next ch-5 space, ch 2; join with dc to first sc – 24 ch-5 spaces.

Round 10: Ch 1, sc in same ch-5 space, ch 4, sc in next ch-5 space, ch 4, *[sc, ch 4] 2 times in corner ch-5 space, [sc in next ch-5 space, ch 4] 5 times; repeat from * around, ending last repeat with [sc in next ch-5 space, ch 4] 3 times; join with slip st to first sc – 28 ch-4 spaces. Fasten off **C**.

Weave in all ends.

NAVY OCTAGON
(continued from page 23)

Round 7: Ch 6 (counts as dc and ch 3), *dc in next dc, ch 2, skip next (ch 2, cluster), (2-dc cluster, ch 3, 2-dc cluster) in next ch-3 space, ch 2, skip next (cluster, ch 2)**, dc in next dc, ch 3; repeat from * around, ending last repeat at **; join with slip st to 3rd ch of beginning ch-6. Fasten off **C**.

Weave in all ends.

ROUNDED SQUARE
(continued from page 25)

Round 8: Join **A** with sc in any corner ch-1 space; ch 1, sc in same space, *[ch 1, skip next dc, sc in next dc] 12 times, ch 1, skip next dc**, [sc, ch 1, sc] in corner ch-1 space; repeat from * around, ending last repeat at **; join with slip st to first sc – 56 sc. Fasten off **A**.

Weave in all ends.

GENERAL INSTRUCTIONS

Abbreviations and Symbols

Here are common crochet abbreviations and symbols including those used in this booklet.

A, B, C	Color A, B, C
ch(s)	chain(s)
cm	centimeters
dc	double crochet(s)
dc2tog	double crochet 2 together
dc3tog	double crochet 3 together
hdc	half double crochet(s)
mm	millimeters
sc	single crochet(s)
st(s)	stitch(es)
tog	together
tr	triple or treble crochet(s)
yo	yarn over

( ) or [ ] — work directions in parentheses or brackets the number of times specified.
* or ** — repeat whatever follows the * or ** as indicated.

Gauge

Gauge refers to the number of stitches and rows in a given area. When making motifs, the gauge is given in the pattern for the size of the motif or for a certain number of rounds. When making projects, ensure that your project is the correct finished size and is to gauge. Working the area as stated in the pattern and then measure to check that it agrees with the gauge given. If it is not the same size, change your hook size. If motif is too large, use a smaller hook. If motif is too small, use a larger hook size.

Joining With Sc

When instructed to join with a sc, begin with a slip knot on the hook. Insert the hook into the stitch or space indicated, yo and pull up a loop, yo and draw through both loops on hook.

Joining With Dc

When instructed to join with a dc, begin with a slip knot on the hook. Yo, holding the loop on the hook, insert the hook into the stitch or space indicated, yo and pull up a loop (3 loops on hook), (yo and draw through 2 loops on hook) twice.

Back Bar

Work only in loops indicated by arrows (Fig. 1).

Fig. 1

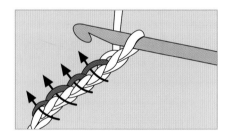

Back Or Front Loop Only

Work only in loop(s) indicated by arrow (Fig. 2).

Fig. 2

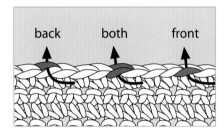

CROCHET TERMINOLOGY		
UNITED STATES		INTERNATIONAL
slip stitch (slip st)	=	single crochet (sc)
single crochet (sc)	=	double crochet (dc)
half double crochet (hdc)	=	half treble crochet (htr)
double crochet (dc)	=	treble crochet(tr)
treble crochet (tr)	=	double treble crochet (dtr)
double treble crochet (dtr)	=	triple treble crochet (ttr)
triple treble crochet (tr tr)	=	quadruple treble crochet (qtr)
skip	=	miss

■□□□ BEGINNER	Projects for first-time crocheters using basic stitches. Minimal shaping.
■■□□ EASY	Projects using yarn with basic stitches, repetitive stitch patterns, simple color changes, and simple shaping and finishing.
■■■□ INTERMEDIATE	Projects using a variety of techniques, such as basic lace patterns or color patterns, mid-level shaping and finishing.
■■■■ EXPERIENCED	Projects with intricate stitch patterns, techniques and dimension, such as non-repeating patterns, multi-color techniques, fine threads, small hooks, detailed shaping and refined finishing.

Changing Colors

Work the last stitch to within one step of completion, hook new yarn *(Fig. 3)* and draw through all loops on the hook.

Fig. 3

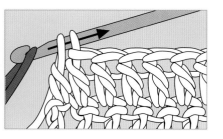

Working In Space Between Stitches

When instructed to work in a space between stitches, insert hook into space indicated by arrow *(Fig. 4)*.

Fig. 4

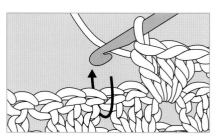

Yarn Weight Symbol & Names	LACE ⓪	SUPER FINE ①	FINE ②	LIGHT ③	MEDIUM ④	BULKY ⑤	SUPER BULKY ⑥
Type of Yarns in Category	Fingering, 10-count crochet thread	Sock, Fingering Baby	Sport, Baby	DK, Light Worsted	Worsted, Afghan, Aran	Chunky, Craft, Rug	Bulky, Roving
Crochet Gauge* Ranges in Single Crochet to 4" (10 cm)	32-42 double crochets**	21-32 sts	16-20 sts	12-17 sts	11-14 sts	8-11 sts	5-9 sts
Advised Hook Size Range	Steel*** 6,7,8 Regular hook B-1	B-1 to E-4	E-4 to 7	7 to I-9	I-9 to K-10.5	K-10.5 to M-13	M-13 and larger

*GUIDELINES ONLY: The chart above reflects the most commonly used gauges and hook sizes for specific yarn categories.

** Lace weight yarns are usually crocheted on larger-size hooks to create lacy openwork patterns. Accordingly, a gauge range is difficult to determine. Always follow the gauge stated in your pattern.

*** Steel crochet hooks are sized differently from regular hooks–the higher the number the smaller the hook, which is the reverse of regular hook sizing.

CROCHET HOOKS															
U.S.	B-1	C-2	D-3	E-4	F-5	G-6	H-8	I-9	J-10	K-10½	L-11	M/N-13	N/P-15	P/Q	Q	S
Metric - mm	2.25	2.75	3.25	3.5	3.75	4	5	5.5	6	6.5	8	9	10	15	16	19

YARN INFORMATION

The projects in this book were created with **RED HEART® SOFT®** yarn.
For best results, we recommend following the pattern exactly as written.

4 RED HEART® Soft®, Art. E728
available in 5 oz (140 g),
256 yd (234 m) balls.

Tips for Washing RED HEART® Soft®:

- Use gentle fabric detergent, such as Ivory®, in warm water.
- Use less than half of the suggested amount of liquid fabric softener, as too much softener will cause fiber to stretch.
- Tumble dry on low and remove from the dryer before completely dry.
- To keep fringe or pompoms looking their best, handwash, lay flat to dry.

For more ideas & inspiration

www.redheart.com • www.facebook.com/redheartyarns

www.pinterest.com/redheartyarns • www.twitter.com/redheartyarns

www.youtube.com/redheartyarns • Instagram @redheartyarns